Open Learning Guide 6

# How to Communicate with the Learner: making the package easy to use

Roger Lewis and Nigel Paine

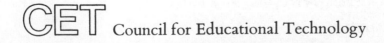
CET Council for Educational Technology

Published and distributed by the Council for Educational Technology, 3 Devonshire Street, London W1N 2BA

First published 1985
ISBN 0 86184–150–6

Lewis, Roger, *1944-*
    How to communicate with the learner: making the package easy to use. — (Open learning guide; 6)
    1. Text-books — Authorship   2. Distance education
    I. Title.   II. Paine, Nigel   III. Council for Educational Technology for the United Kingdom   IV. Series
    373.3'2    LB3045.5

ISBN 0 86184–150–6

Printed in Great Britain by H Charlesworth & Co Ltd
254 Deighton Road
Huddersfield HD2 1JJ

# How to Communicate with the Learner

# Contents

# *Preface*

Since 1975 the Council for Educational Technology has been continuously involved in the development of open-learning systems. The first stages of this work concentrated on 'non-advanced further education' and enabled the Council to make a major contribution to the National Extension College's 'FlexiStudy' system and other early developments, and incidentally to provide much advice and practical help in the form of publications and training workshops to lecturers who were finding their way into the new field of open learning. This experience (allied to that of the Open University) helped to provide the foundation upon which the 'Open Tech' programme (Manpower Services Commission) and PICKUP initiative (Department of Education and Science) are built, has led to the much more flexible approach now being taken by the Business and Technician Education Council and other validating bodies, and is recognized by the contract given to the Council by MSC to provide a training and support unit for Open Tech projects.

Maintaining the momentum of its work in open learning, the Council has moved into the fields of supported self-study in secondary schools and informal adult learning. In all this work over the past nine years, the Council has benefited from the cooperation and personal experience of an increasingly large group of experienced specialists in open learning and has, through its publications, attempted to make this experience available to lecturers, trainers and teachers who found themselves confronted with the need to get involved in open-learning methods.

This new series of Open Learning Guides is a further move in making the accumulated experience of those who have developed open-learning methods in the United Kingdom available to newcomers to the field. The series editor, Roger Lewis, has taken a lead in developments both through his work for the National Extension College and through his involvement from the beginning with the Council's own work. The drafts of the Guides have been commented on and improved by a process of consultation with several experts in the open-learning network, with the intention that the result will be a series of books which are directly helpful to those in industry, the professions, and adult, further and higher education who are called upon to develop and run open-learning schemes.

Norman Willis
Assistant Director
Council for Educational Technology
April 1984

*Introduction*

# Introduction

**THE OPEN-LEARNING GUIDES**
This series of books is intended as a practical help to people setting up open-learning schemes whether in education or training. The advice is deliberately aimed across the whole range of schemes and levels. The structure of the series is as follows.

| WHAT IS OPEN LEARNING? |
| --- |

| OPEN LEARNING IN ACTION: CASE-STUDIES |
| --- |

| HOW TO DEVELOP AND MANAGE AN OPEN-LEARNING SCHEME | HOW TO TUTOR AND SUPPORT LEARNERS | HOW TO FIND AND ADAPT MATERIALS AND CHOOSE MEDIA |
| --- | --- | --- |

| HOW TO HELP LEARNERS ASSESS THEIR PROGRESS: HOW TO WRITE OBJECTIVES, SELF-ASSESSMENT QUESTIONS AND ACTIVITIES |
| --- |

| HOW TO COMMUNICATE WITH THE LEARNER |
| --- |

| HOW TO MANAGE THE PRODUCTION PROCESS |
| --- |

The Guides thus cover the three main parts of most schemes: a management system, a tutorial support system and learning materials. Each book stands on its own but there are many areas of overlap and reference is made to other volumes in the series. In particular you are recommended to consult Volume 1, *Open Learning in Action,* when you use this text.

All the volumes except *Open Learning in Action* contain open-learning features. These include:

— objectives
— quiz sections which act as summaries
— activities to enable you to apply your learning to your work
— checklists to guide you whilst working through the activities
— job aids to use in running your scheme
— the provision of frequent examples to show how the ideas have been applied in particular cases.

These features are indicated in the text by introductory symbols to make them easily recognizable. *Key words for this volume are defined in the Glossary in Section 7.*

### WHAT THIS BOOK COVERS

The learner in an open scheme is distinguished from more conventional students in a variety of ways. He is

— learning away from an 'expert'
— fitting learning in with other activities such as employment
— isolated at least to some degree from fellow learners and/or a learning centre
— likely to be older.

It follows that a larger weight must fall upon the learning resources than, say, a textbook would be asked to carry in a more conventional course. The open-learning package has to incorporate the methods used by the teacher/tutor with the group. It must do more than simply present content to the learner; it must include the interactive features of good teaching.

This book follows through the implications of this. It helps you to choose, or to write, material that enables the learner to

— find those parts of the package he wants
— pace himself
— interact with the material
— develop his own learning style
— grow in independence.

We offer guidelines on how to achieve this. The guidelines should be adapted for the particular use you have in mind. It is not possible to lay down hard and fast rules in an area developing as quickly as open learning.

### Objectives

After using this book you should be able to

— identify ways in which a package can support learning (see Section One)

— include support features in your package (see Section One)
— design the package to take account of learners with different abilities, experience, needs and learning styles (see Section Two)
— structure a package to make it easy to use (see Section Two)
— establish, and maintain, a high level of learner activity whilst working through your package (see Section Three)
— write readable prose (see Section Three)
— use opportunities for illustration (see Section Four)
— carry out any responsibilities you have for (a) the format and (b) the layout of a package (see Section Five)
— make a start on writing (see Section Six).

You will find detailed objectives at the beginning of each section.

When we use the word 'writing' you should take this to include the equivalent activity in another medium, eg, preparing an audio script or storyboard.

The emphasis throughout is practical. You should treat the book as a job aid, carrying out those activities relevant to your own context and using the checklists to guide decision-making.

**ACKNOWLEDGEMENTS**
A team of readers very helpfully commented on this book in draft. The readers were:

John Coffey
Rob Littlejohn
Gaye Manwaring

Phil Race
Frances Robertson
Doug Spencer
Philip Waterhouse

The authors would particularly like to thank Gaye Manwaring and Clive Neville for their detailed help and Janet Bollen for dealing with the many changes made to the manuscript.

Bob Windsor, Clive Neville and Lesley MacDonald managed the project for CET and Muriel Brooks edited this and other volumes in the series. The authors would like to thank them for their ready cooperation at all times.

Roger Lewis
Nigel Paine
February 1985

*Section One. What's So Special About Open
Learning?*

# What's So Special About Open Learning?

INTRODUCTION
Open-learning materials are designed to be used by learners working on their own. What are the implications of this? We shall look first at what a good class teacher does; then at how good classroom practice can be incorporated in open-learning materials.

## Objectives
When you have worked through this section you should be able to

— recognize ways in which an effective teacher/trainer facilitates learning in a conventional class
— identify ways in which support to learning can be built into a package
— include these features in your own open-learning materials.

LEARNING IN A CONVENTIONAL CLASS
In a well-run conventional classroom the teacher manages at least two processes. (Here and in what follows we use the terms 'teacher' and 'classroom'. What is said applies equally to lecturing or training. Please substitute for 'teacher' and 'classroom' whichever are the appropriate words in your own context.) He transmits the content of the course, and he helps the learners to absorb and use this content. The second of these two processes is vital: the successful teacher spends a good deal of time helping students to learn. What, more specifically, does he do to support them?

We can pick out many ways the good teacher uses to help learning to occur. He

— arouses interest
— makes objectives clear
— structures the content
— gives practice and feedback on the practice
— attends to the difficult and unfamiliar
— establishes two-way communication.

This section looks at each of these.

9

### Arousing interest

The teacher finds interesting ways of presenting his subject. He relates it to the needs of his learners — such as the need to know, to manage life better, to master a skill to be used at work, to pass an examination. He knows that he must catch the learner's attention. At the beginning of a lesson he will be welcoming, putting learners at their ease and promising a stimulating time. He will be businesslike but informal. When a class is made up of disparate learners the teacher may spend a good deal of time 'breaking the ice', even using role plays or relaxation exercises. Such time pays off later, in terms of stronger commitment from the learners and group solidarity.

> 'The machine can store details of any kind — your football team's scores, your spending, phone numbers of your friends. That's what we'll look at today, with plenty of examples. You'll be able to program the computer with instructions you want it to carry out. OK. So let's get on. Right Brian, you're interested in . . .'

### Making objectives clear

The teacher explains clearly where the lesson is leading. He sets out those skills and capacities the learner can expect to acquire. These are the objectives or outcomes of the lesson.

> 'This lesson deals with vertebrates. When you've finished it you should be able to list four main characteristics . . .'

He also explains any knowledge the learner should have before tackling the session, ie, any prerequisites.

> 'You'll need to remember how to take the top plate off. If you've forgotten, or if you were away when we did it, then take out a worksheet and follow the instructions. I'll come and check your work before you move on.'

The good teacher is flexible, adapting content and methods to suit an individual learner.

> 'Jim, you may find it easier to go straight to the system descriptions in Chapter 3 and return to fundamentals of programming later. You might try it this way . . .'

### Structuring the content

The teacher decides the best way of sequencing content, to make learning easier. He attends to the shape both of the whole course and of each part of it. He carefully 'signposts' the learner indicating

— where he has got to
— what will come next
— the links between different topics.

Each lesson has shape — a clear beginning and end.

'You remember the module on the new switchboard. Well, now we're going to look at another use of technology in the office.'

'We've spent several weeks now on wordprocessing. You've tried out two different packages. But how might the average secretary *use* this new technology? We are going to move on to that now. I want to look at a typical office and show three main ways in which wordprocessing makes the secretary's job easier.'

## Giving practice

The good teacher gives the learner plenty of chances to practise. This helps both teacher and learner assess how far the objectives are being met. It helps the learner to apply new knowledge and skills. The teacher

— asks questions
— sets activities
— gives exercises.

'I've designed a worksheet to help you to check your understanding of this part of the course.'

He goes on to provide feedback in the form of

— answers
— commentary on performance
— review discussions.

'Your solutions to the first two questions are fine but in the third you have ignored the fact that . . .'

He will also give any necessary advice on procedures the learner should carry out in order to practise, directing attention to key stages or questions.

'It's a difficult passage and I don't want you to worry about all the details. Skim-read it and then make notes only on major points. For example pay close attention to . . .'

## Attending to the difficult and unfamiliar

The teacher will identify those parts of the material that learners regularly find difficult. These might include skills, attitudes and new concepts. He uses techniques to help the learner tackle such difficult areas, for example returning frequently to them and illustrating them by

— reference to familiar experiences.

> 'You know when you start the car with the headlights on, they go dim and then recover . . . Well, that's basically the same process as we have here . . .'

— providing extra practice

> 'Try again, using these figures.'

— careful questioning

> 'Why did you get angry with Stephanie at that particular moment?'

He uses examples and analogies and he gives reassurance and encouragement. The good teacher allows the learner the chance to express the difficulties he is meeting and he accepts them as valid.

> 'Which of these concepts do you find most difficult, John . . . Yes, I agree it's hard going at present, but once we can understand and explain the relationships between rhythm, rhyme and metre the rest of the course falls into place.'

The good teacher is also prepared to listen to the learners' views, including — if necessary — accepting criticism.

> 'I didn't feel that lesson was particularly successful. You seemed to have a lot of problems with it. Let's work out what went wrong.'

## Establishing two-way communication
The extracts so far may have given the impression that communication is one-way, from transmitting teacher to receiving learners. This is not the case: communication is two-way and the good teacher listens as much as he talks.

| Transmitting | Choice of appropriate language and tone |
| --- | --- |
| | Selection of the right examples |
| | Anecdotes; experiences |
| | Use of non-verbal cues such as facial expression and gesture |
| Receiving | Listening attentively |
| | Showing interest |
| | Looking at the learner |
| | Appearing relaxed |

So in the successful classroom the teacher does much more than transmit content. He also supports learning by

— arousing interest
— making objectives clear
— structuring the material
— giving practice and feedback
— attending to the difficult
— establishing two-way communication.

Observation of good teachers shows that a surprisingly high percentage of their time is spent supporting learning in these ways.

### OPEN-LEARNING MATERIALS

In open learning the tutor is rarely available to provide these forms of support at first hand. Contact may be possible, but usually only infrequently. Some schemes launch learners with a face-to-face session deliberately intended to create camaraderie and build morale. But as courses grow more modularized and the entry points are more diverse this becomes increasingly difficult.

We are led to this conclusion: the forms of support provided in classroom interaction have to be built into the learning materials themselves. The materials thus become sources both of content and of support. Equivalents have to be found for the good teaching practices outlined in the previous section.

The table on page 14 sets out the forms of support which the package should include. We also add a note of where, in this volume, you can find a discussion of each.

We are thus talking about something much more sophisticated than a textbook. Textbooks generally try to cover only one of the two components so far discussed: content, not support. Textbooks are organized according to the logic of the subject rather than the logic of learning. They take the perspective of the subject specialist rather than that of the learner. They require the physical presence and support of a teacher. Open-learning materials are more complex in structure and function. This point is made by Philip Waterhouse when discussing open learning in schools:

'*The pupil is provided with learning materials that have been very carefully chosen for self-study.* Ideally these would be multi-media. Such materials would be well structured and carefully sequenced; they would emphasize objectives, provide guidance about learning strategies, give plenty of practice, suggest things to do, and through self-assessment questions give feedback to the pupil. The materials may be completely self-contained in one package — specially created for self-study. Alternatively, the resource materials and the guidance to the learner may be packaged separately. The resources would provide the data and stimuli; and the guidance would provide task cards or study guides, assessment tests, and problems' (*Supported Self-Study: a handbook for teachers,* Waterhouse, 1983, p 9).

The difference between textbooks and open-learning materials can be summarized as in the table on page 15.

| Form of support | Where covered |
|---|---|
| Transmits content — clearly, logically and by using a varied approach | Section 2 How to construct flexible packages<br>Section 3 Writing for learning |
| Arouses and maintains interest | Section 3 Writing for learning<br>Section 4 Illustrations<br>Section 5 Format and layout |
| Makes objective clear | (See note below) |
| Structures the content for learning | Section 2 How to construct flexible packages<br>Section 3 Writing for learning<br>Section 6 How to get started |
| Provides practice and feedback | Section 2 How to construct flexible packages<br>Section 3 Writing for learning<br>Section 5 Format and layout<br>Section 6 How to get started |
| Tackles difficult material positively | Section 3 Writing for learning |
| Establishes two-way communication | Section 3 Writing for learning<br>Section 4 Illustrations<br>Section 5 Format and layout |

*Note*

Volume 2 of the Open Learning Guides (*How to Help Learners Assess Their Progress: writing objectives, self-assessment questions and activities*) is relevant throughout and especially on making objectives clear, giving practice and feedback, and establishing two-way communication.

Volume 8 (*How to Find and Adapt Materials and Select Media*) is also relevant. It shows you how to check other packages to see whether they have these forms of support, how to adapt packages to include the necessary features, and how to use media to support learners.

The first half of Volume 5 (*How to Develop and Manage an Open-Learning Scheme*) is relevant to all the issues. *Open Learning in Action* (Volume 1) shows how, in practice, actual open-learning schemes include these features in their materials.

| Textbooks | Open-learning materials |
|---|---|
| Assume interest | Arouse interest |
| Written for teacher use | Written for learner use |
| Designed for a wide market | Designed for identified groups |
| Rarely give objectives | Always give objectives |
| One route through | Many routes through |
| Structured according to logic of the content | Structured according to needs of learner |
| Little or no self-assessment | Major emphasis on self-assessment |
| Ignore likely learner difficulties | Address learner difficulties |
| Rarely offer summaries | Always offer summaries |
| Impersonal style | Personal style |
| Dense in content | Content unpacked |
| Densely packed appearance | Well-spaced-out appearance |
| Packaged for sale | Packaged for use |
| No mechanism to collect learner views | Learners' evaluation sought |
| No study skills advice | Provide study skills advice |

The lists in the table suggest two opposed products. There is, of course, a grey area, eg, the textbook that includes some of the features of the open-learning package. See *How to Find and Adapt Materials and Select Media* (Volume 8) for further discussion of the range of materials that may be used in an open-learning scheme.

**Activity**

Choose one of the following options. Use as a guide the checklist printed below; adapt it if necessary.

*1. If you are choosing a package from those already prepared*
Review the packages from the point of view of this section.

*2. If you are preparing an open-learning package*
Decide how you will embody within your package the forms of support outlined in this section.

## Checklist

*Content*

Is the content presented logically, from a learning point of view?

Is it presented in an interesting and varied way?

*Support*

Is the package likely to raise and maintain the learner's interest?

Are the objectives of the package defined? Are they clear?

Is the package structured well? Is there diagnostic testing? Provision for routeing? (See Section Two for these and other structural features.)

Is the learner given practice and feedback?

Have you provided any necessary help on procedures or study strategies?

Are likely difficulties acknowledged and dealt with? Are there enough examples?

Is there an opportunity for the learner to give his views of the package?

Is the package attractively presented? Easy to use and handle?

Is the language welcoming?

*Section Two. How to Construct Flexible Packages*

# How to Construct Flexible Packages

**INTRODUCTION: WHY MAKE THE PACKAGE FLEXIBLE?**
No two learners are alike. Each learner is an individual and just as the good teacher caters for each individual so too should a learning package. Learners differ in

— ability and experience
— needs, wants and purposes
— learning styles.

The package designer has to find ways of catering for these differences. This section suggests some ways.

☐O **Objectives**
When you have worked through this section you should be able to

—structure your package to provide for different learner starting points; different routes through the package; users with different learning styles
— design a package in manageable chunks for the learner
— decide how to begin and end each chunk
— provide in-text aids such as headings and other signposts to help the learner organize his study.

**HOW TO PROVIDE FOR DIFFERENT STARTING-POINTS**

**According to ability**
A diagnostic test can help different learners to locate their starting-point on the course. Someone already expert in a particular topic should not need to work through a module covering it; a pre-test can confirm his knowledge and help him to find a more appropriate starting-point. On the other hand the starting-point of a package may be too advanced for another learner who may lack certain necessary skills and thus need to be steered to a different package altogether, or helped to gain the relevant experience by some other means.

This can be shown diagrammatically.

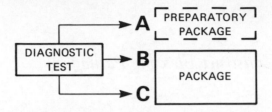

The diagnostic test shows that learner A needs an earlier package; learner B is ready to begin where the package itself begins; learner C can start at a point further on in the package.

Volume 2, *How to Help Learners Assess Their Progress: writing objectives, self-assessment questions and activities,* gives advice on how to write the kinds of question that may be used in a diagnostic test.

### According to purpose
The above example presupposes a sequential course, a series of chunks each of which relies upon knowledge of the previous ones. Not all courses are organized in this way. There may be a group of chunks, each of which is self-contained and no one of which is more or less difficult than the others. In this case a diagnostic test helps the learner to define which chunk he needs. This pattern is used in some of the projects resourced by the Manpower Services Commission's Open Tech Programme, where learners are using packages for updating purposes.

In the example below the diagnostic test shows the learner that Module D is the one most likely to match his purpose.

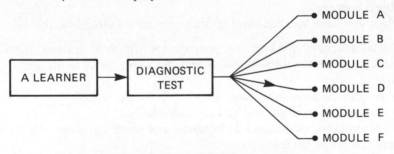

(Note: in this example the chunks are called 'modules'. For terminology, see the Glossary on page 117.)

##### HOW TO PROVIDE FOR DIFFERENT ROUTES
### According to ability
The previous section dealt with ways of helping learners to start the package at a point appropriate to their abilities or previous experience. This section shows how the writer can provide different routes through the package. Again, we are assuming that the package is divided into chunks called 'modules'. We'll look first at possible movements through a package which has its modules sequenced, with each module building on the previous one. Note: in the diagram on page 21 we have used the

word 'fail' as shorthand for 'mastery not yet achieved' or 'module not relevant to learner need'.

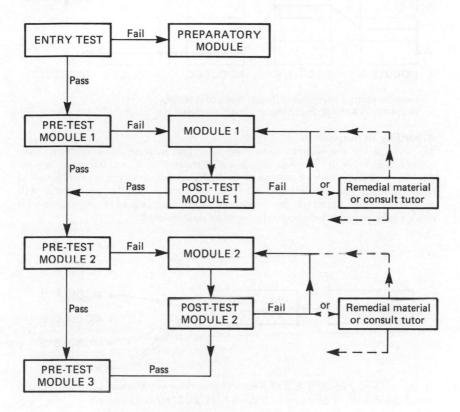

The structure shown in the diagram depends on a series of tests. On entry to the package the learner takes a test. If he passes (however 'pass' is defined) then he moves into the pre-test for module 1. If he passes that then he skips module 1 and moves on to the pre-test for module 2. The module pre-test is thus an indication of whether or not the learner needs that module. If he passes, then he has already achieved mastery and so can move on, leapfrogging the module itself. If he does not pass the pre-test then he works through that module and takes a post-test. Success in that means that he moves to the pre-test for the following module. If he fails the post-test then there has to be some further provision — to go through the module again, to work through some fresh material, or to consult the tutor. The tutor may advise the learner to move back, or move forward, or he may provide further new material. Ideally the pre-tests also enable the learner to select from within the module. If, for example, the learner gets questions 3 and 4 completely correct but has difficulty with 1, 2 and 5, then he should be steered only to those sections of the module that deal with areas in which he has not yet achieved mastery (1, 2 and 5). Another approach to routeing is shown in the diagram on page 22.

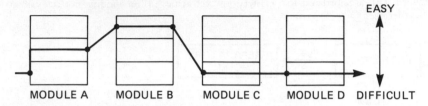

Modules each of which has different levels of difficulty;
each ● marks a test with consequent routeing directions.

## According to purpose

The example in the diagram shows modules that increase in complexity. Each module is built on the previous one: 1 is a prerequisite of 2, etc. But as we saw on page 20, a package may be structured according to different principles. Modules of equal difficulty may be distinguished from one another only by the topic or skill which they cover. In this case instead of pre-tests some other kind of diagnostic tool is needed to help the learner choose the topics or skills he needs.

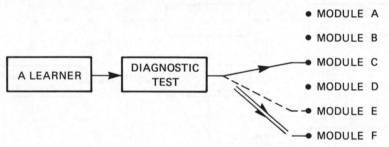

In this example, Module F is the most urgent priority; Module C would be very useful; Module E — do if time; Modules A, B and D are not necessary.

A different learner might take modules A and C as priorities with module D as a useful further resource if time were available.

### HOW TO PROVIDE FOR DIFFERENT LEARNING STYLES

So different learners might need different routes through the package. The writer can provide a map to help them. This is part of the flexibility of use that the writer needs to build into the learning materials. These days a package is seen as a resource for learners to use in whatever ways they feel appropriate. In the bad old days of 'correspondence education' there was one route only. Learners who skipped a module could find it impossible to proceed; learners who missed out questions were made to feel that they had cheated. In fact such strategies on the part of the learner are often very sensible. We all learn in different ways and find different features of a package useful. A package should thus be capable of use by learners who employ a variety of strategies.

We'll use an example to make this clear. As printed, the structure of our imaginary module is as shown in the diagram on page 23. This module can be used in a variety

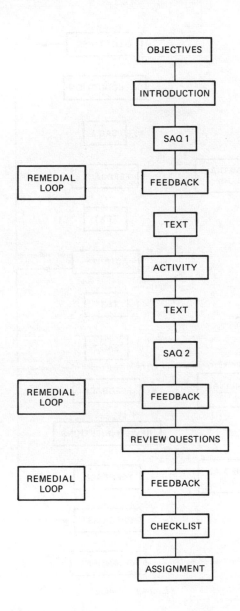

of ways to arrive at the same learning outcomes. The variety is infinite — even without adding extra media to what is a simple print package. We shall show just five learner routes through the package.

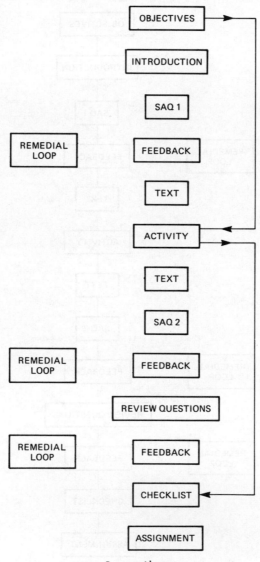

*Learner 1's route*

*Learner 1* looks at objectives, then goes straight to the activity. After he has carried out the activity he moves on to the checklist to see if he has forgotten anything. Learner 1 is keen to put the objectives into practice as quickly as possible.

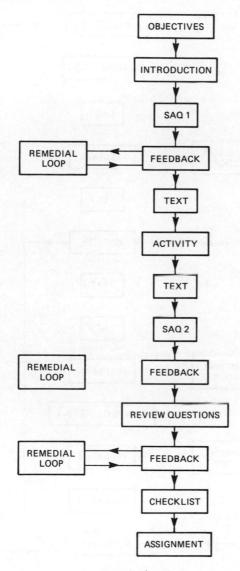

*Learner 2's route*

*Learner 2* moves systematically through the module exactly as it stands. He also takes two remedial loops, once after SAQ 1 where the feedback perhaps shows him that he has not yet mastered the relevant objective; again after the review questions. Learner 2 is thorough and likes to use every possible aid to learning.

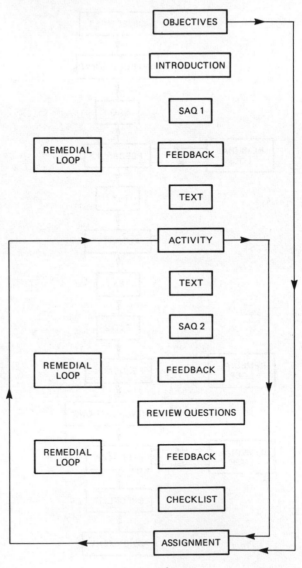

*Learner 3's route*

*Learner 3* begins with the objectives and then looks carefully at the assignment. He doubles back in order to carry out the activity, perhaps because he thinks this will better prepare him for the assignment which he then does. Learner 3 treats contact with the tutor as a priority.

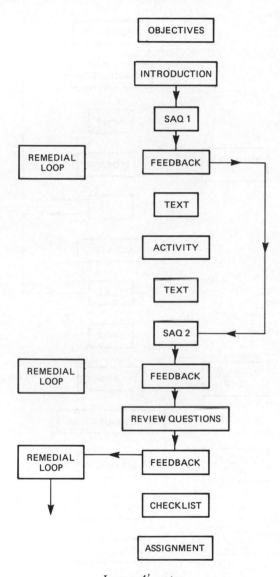

*Learner 4's route*

*Learner 4* goes to the introduction first, then to SAQ 1 and its associated feedback. Learner 4 seems to like using in-text questions because he moves straight through from SAQ 1 to SAQ 2 and then to the review questions at the end of the unit. He gets one of the review questions wrong so takes the remedial loop.

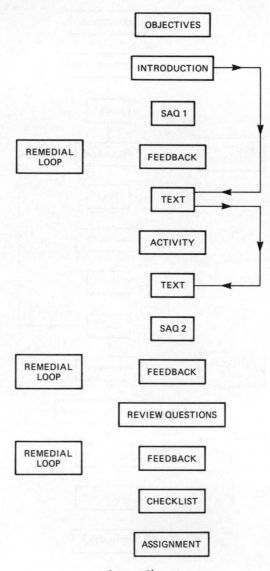

*Learner 5's route*

*Learner 5* also starts with the introduction. This learner is rather traditional. He reads only the sections of straight text and seems to learn from these without any further support.

The point to note is that the structure allows equal access to learners with different styles and preferences. How they use the material will depend on who they are, the nature of the subject, their previous experience or knowledge and their reasons for studying. It is the author's responsibility to make the package as accessible as possible to learners who use different styles.

One of the weaknesses of programmed learning was that it catered for only one learning style. It left no flexibility for people wishing to develop alternative styles of learning. It therefore never won general acceptance. It would be unwise to recreate the limitations of programmed learning when developing open-learning packages in print or, as is more likely, in a computer-based package. (See *Open Learning and Information Technology: the interactivity analogue* by Paine in the Booklist.)

## Activity

If you are selecting a ready-made package:
— review it against the checklist given below.

If you are preparing a package decide:

— how you will help learners to start the package at an appropriate point
— how you will help learners to find appropriate routes through the material
— how you will cater for a variety of learning styles.

Use as a guide the checklist below.

## Checklist

Have you helped learners decide at which point they should start
— by a pre-test
— by some other diagnostic aid?

Once started, can the learner route himself through the package
— by testing
— by some other aid?

Does your package contain remedial and enrichment loops?

Can the learner enter, use and leave the package with ease?

Have you explained different ways in which the package may be used?

### HOW TO DESIGN A PACKAGE

By now, you will be aware that the package should be organized in a way that makes flexible use possible. Learners will have different levels of experience and ability. They will approach the package with different purposes. They will employ different learning styles. In this part we consider in more detail how you can design the necessary flexibility into a package. We cover

— ways of dividing the material into manageable chunks for learning
— ways of beginning each chunk
— ways of ending each chunk
— in-text aids
— guides to a package.

### Chunking

A package will have to be divided in some way into its component parts. Here is one possible way of doing it.

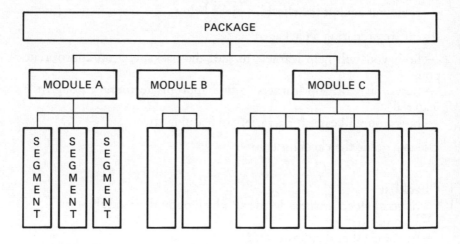

Note that other terms may be used for the above levels, eg, 'course' instead of 'package', 'unit' instead of 'module', 'section' or 'chapter' instead of segment.

It is also possible to subdivide a package further, eg, in the above we could have another level within the 'segment' called, let's say, 'section'. How many pages and learning-hours are included at each level (module, segment, etc,) will depend on the scheme. (Section Six shows one way of planning this.) But let's assume that a segment in the above design is planned to take the learner approximately one study-hour. Module C would then look like this.

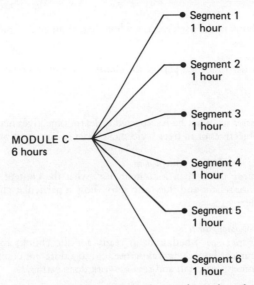

(Some of the segments in the above example are themselves further divided into approximately 20-minute study periods.) The advantage of chunking in this way is that the learner can easily plan his study. He can use the package in a variety of contexts. Sometimes he will have only a short time available; at others he'll be able to settle down at a desk; he may be on a bus or at work. If he can easily see how long a particular chunk will take, and what kind of work is required, he can then pick out a part of the package relevant to his circumstances at the time.

You may divide your own material in very different ways to that shown in the above illustration. Much will depend on the nature of your learners and the subject or skills you are teaching; but whatever system you adopt you should remember to break the content into manageable sections for your learners.

Each self-contained chunk of the package will need a beginning, middle and end. In the example above this would be the levels of segment, module and package. A one-hour segment, a six-hour module and (say) a 30-hour package would each need these features to give coherence at all levels. The rest of this part of the book suggests features you can use at each of these points, to help a learner organize his study. In what follows we consider

— features to open a chunk
— features inside the chunk
— features to end a chunk.

## Beginnings

There are many ways of helping the learner to get into a chunk. Each way listed below serves a slightly different purpose; for example, a statement of objectives performs a different task from a contents list. There is overlap between the features but don't worry about this. If you decide to use several you will enable the learner to choose his own personal best way in. (Remember what we said earlier about different learning strategies.)

*Chunk title/number*
This locates the chunk in the package as a whole (eg, segment 3 of module B).

*Contents list*
This helps the learner find each part of the chunk and it shows relationships between parts.

*List of objectives*
This helps the learner see what he is expected to learn; objectives may be in the form of conventional objectives or in freer style, eg, a series of key questions.

*Outline (note form); introduction; concept map*
These show, in more detail than a contents list, what the content is, and how the different aspects interrelate; and they also show how a particular chunk fits into the package as a whole.

*List of prerequisites or diagnostic test*
This helps the learner see whether he is ready for the chunk; routes the learner according to his current knowledge/expertise, eg, to a different chunk, to a remedial chunk or to enrichment material; and revises work done earlier.

*Pre-test*
This helps the learner to see how much of the chunk he already knows, and which parts of it to study.

*List of anything the learner needs to hand, eg, special equipment or textbooks*
This makes it possible for the learner to work without interruption and frustration.

*Indication of the time the chunk should take*
This helps the learner to plan his study, eg, when, where and for what periods.

The following examples show different ways to begin a chunk. You may like to check how many of the above features are included.

---

10

Before starting to use this manual, answer as many questions as you can of Test B in the Test Booklet.

This will give you some idea of what the manual is about and help you recognise the main points when you see them.

Once you have completed the questions, have the answers checked by your tutor, manager, training officer or instructor.

You will need to have with you all the items of equipment and materials listed on the next page before you continue with this manual.

11

```
The items you will need to use while studying this manual are:

        Cassette tape player
        35 mm slide viewer
        Notepad and pencil

When you have obtained these items, turn the page and commence
MODULE 1.
```

*Extract from 'Self-Instruction Manual' Die Cutting — 1. Principles', pp 10, 11, published by and reproduced by permission of the British Fibreboard Packaging Employers Association*

# UNIT 15

 **WRITING**

Letters III
Opinion

The last section dealing with the writing of letters considers those expressing opinions.

 **READING AND UNDERSTANDING**

Summary

Although not essential for the examination, this guide on how to summarize should help in the comprehension question.

 **READING LIST**

Some collections of letters you may find interesting.

 **VOCABULARY**

A look at some words used in an editorial from *The Listener*.

 **LANGUAGE**

Jargon and Clichés

An examination of the words and phrases that come into these categories.

 **SPELLING**

How knowing prefixes and suffixes can help your spelling.

*Extract from 'A New English Course' by Rhodri Jones, p 135, published by Heinemann Educational Books in conjunction with the National Extension College, and reproduced by permission of the National Extension College*

# Introduction to
# Telecommunication Systems R1   <small>SCOTEC</small>

SECTION: **A**

LESSON: **1**

---

**LAST LESSON**

NONE

---

**THIS LESSON**

**THE TRANSFER OF INFORMATION**

**OBJECTIVE**

When you have completed this lesson you will be able to describe
communication systems in terms of transmitter, medium and
receiver.

---

**NEXT LESSON**

SOUND WAVES

---

**CONTENTS**

| TEXT | **520 WORDS** | SAQ |
| FIGURES | 3 | ANSWERS |
| EXAMPLES | | AUDIOTAPE |
| PRACTICAL | | |

© The Post Office 1978                                    Issue 1

---

*Extract from the Scottish Technical Education Council Certificate Programme in Electrical and
Electronic Engineering, Section A, Lesson 2, reproduced by permission of British Telecom*

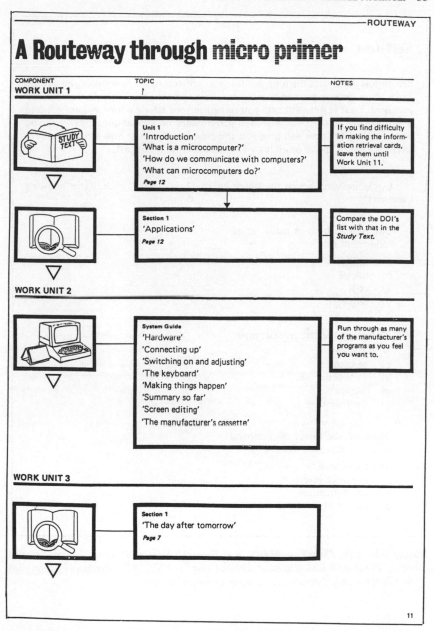

ROUTEWAY

# A Routeway through micro primer

| COMPONENT | TOPIC | NOTES |
| --- | --- | --- |
| **WORK UNIT 1** | | |

**Unit 1**
'Introduction'
'What is a microcomputer?'
'How do we communicate with computers?'
'What can microcomputers do?'
*Page 12*

If you find difficulty in making the information retrieval cards, leave them until Work Unit 11.

**Section 1**
'Applications'
*Page 12*

Compare the DOI's list with that in the *Study Text.*

**WORK UNIT 2**

**System Guide**
'Hardware'
'Connecting up'
'Switching on and adjusting'
'The keyboard'
'Making things happen'
'Summary so far'
'Screen editing'
'The manufacturer's cassette'

Run through as many of the manufacturer's programs as you feel you want to.

**WORK UNIT 3**

**Section 1**
'The day after tomorrow'
*Page 7*

11

*Extract from the Microelectronics Education Programme 'Micro Primer' pack, prepared and edited by Ron Jones, published by Tecmedia (Loughborough), copyright CET*

# Self-test

Before you go on with the unit, do this short self-test to see how much you already know about the way your body functions. If you find the test difficult, don't be discouraged. Your results will help you recognize your strong points and any areas in which you are weak. Your improved performance on similar questions when you have finished the unit will give you the pleasure of seeing how much you have learned. Do not spend more than 15 minutes on this self-test.

Circle the letter beside the statement that best answers each of the following questions.

1. The human body is made up of millions of tiny
   a) organs
   b) nuclei
   c) cells
   d) tissues

2. The air we breathe consists mainly of the gas
   a) oxygen
   b) carbon dioxide
   c) nitrogen
   d) hydrogen

3. Most of the water is removed from the digestive system by
   a) the stomach
   b) the large intestine
   c) the duodenum
   d) the small intestine

*Extract from 'How Does Your Body Get its Energy?', Science 010 Unit 2, Open Learning Institute, PO Box 94 000, Richmond, British Columbia V6Y 2AZ, reproduced by permission of the Open Learning Institute. There are seven further questions.*

**In-text**
The text itself should contain the interactive features at the heart of open learning: self-assessment questions, activities and whatever other means you favour for this purpose. This applies whatever medium is used for the package. A typical chunk could proceed somewhat like this.

(Beginnings)

| | |
|---|---|
| Orientating question/quiz | Attracts learner's attention |
| Text 1 | Provides necessary content |
| Self-assessment question 1 | Enables learner to test his understanding of previous content |
| Discussion of self-assessment question 1 | Enables learner to assess how adequate his response was |
| Text: case-study | Applies content to real-life example |
| Activity and checklist | Helps learner to apply materials to his own situation |
| Text 2 | Provides necessary content |
| Self-assessment question 2 | Enables learner to test his understanding of previous content |
| Discussion of self-assessment question 2 | Enables learner to assess how adequate his responses are |
| Text: example | Applies content to real-life example |
| Cumulative test on text 1 and 2 | Offers learner further chance to check mastery of objectives |

(Endings)

See Volume 2 (*How to Help Learners Assess Their Progress: writing objectives, self-assessment questions and activities*) for a full discussion of objectives, self-assessment questions and activities and related feedback. See also Section Five of this volume for a discussion of how to choose and show format features.

*Headings*
It is difficult to be specific about the number and nature of headings you will need. Much depends on the structure of your chunk — if, for example, you are writing chunks of 30 pages you will use more headings than if your chunk is a third of this length. In longer texts headings are very important in that they help the learner to

— locate a particular subject
— get a feel for the topic area
— see how long each section is likely to take
— get an idea of the sequence.

In addition, they break up the text and make it look attractive. They can act as an invitation to the learner, particularly if they are in the form of questions, as in the following example.

# Contents

*Extract from 'Editing for Everyone' by Celia Hall, p iii, published by and reproduced by permission of the National Extension College*

Sometimes, for example for the purposes of cross-referencing, you will need to number headings. But keep this to a minimum. Some texts produce so many headings and subheadings and such a variety of numbering systems that the overall effect is to confuse the learner, as in the following example.

*Extract from 'The Rise of Christianity' by Francis Clark, p 5, published by the Open University Press and reproduced by permission of the Open University*

Headings make sense only if they are logical. The first responsibility for this lies with the writer. A house style then ensures that the writer's intentions are clearly indicated to the editor and thence to the learner. Headings in the text should be consistent with those in the contents list. Headings in the margins can be a useful device for learners who wish to get a summary of content as they go, or to skim the text for material relevant to their needs. You will have to work out

— how many headings you will need
— how frequently headings will appear
— whether you will use subheadings
— whether you will number your headings
— what style of heading you will use (eg, questions or statements)
— where headings will be positioned.

If you are using a medium other than print the above principles still apply, adapted as necessary.

*Signposting*
Headings serve to reinforce the structure of a chunk but they are rarely enough used on their own. Each chunk is likely to consist of several paragraphs and these will need linking. One chunk will also need linking to another.

> I have given five reasons for a change. Now I'll go through the first of these in more detail.

This kind of signposting orients the learner to where he has come from and where he is going. It is the essence of all good writing, but it is particularly important when writing for someone studying alone.

Different kinds of signposts or 'structuring moves' are set out in the following table.

| Purpose of signpost | Example |
|---|---|
| To describe the structure of what is to follow | 'We will cover the main purposes of a wordprocessing package . . .'<br>'I shall describe three packages . . .' |
| To indicate the beginnings and ends of topics | 'To begin with . . .'<br>'And now we'll look at . . .'<br>'I'll finish this section by giving you the chance to tackle a self-assessment question . . .' |
| To emphasize important points and examples | 'The key point is . . .'<br>'The best example is . . .'<br>'You should remember . . .' |
| To show relationships within the subject matter | 'Because . . .'<br>'So . . .'<br>'It follows that . . .'<br>'However . . .'<br>'But . . .'<br>'So this is where A fits in with B . . .' |

## Endings
You should choose from such features as are listed below.

*Summary of main points, in different words from those used earlier*
This helps the learner consolidate; reassesses the content; and reminds the learner of the routes he has taken.

*Review questions/post-test with responses*
These give the learner a further chance to check how well he has mastered objectives.

*Exercise/assignment sent to a tutor for marking*
This provides the learner with individual comment on his work (see Volume 2, *How to Help Learners Assess Their Progress: writing objectives, self-assessment questions and activities*).

*Checklist of main points/procedures to follow*
This summarizes content; acts as a guide to action; and is useful for revision.

*Ideas on what to do next, eg, while waiting for work to be marked*
These maintain momentum.

*Additional work, eg, reading, practical*
This helps the advanced learner.

*Information about the next topic of study*
This is to arouse interest; to help learners prepare, eg, to get equipment/textbooks ready.

The examples on pages 42–44 show several of these features.

## A guide to the package
In the diagram on page 30 we use the term 'package' to describe a total set of learning materials. You should remember to include the necessary information for this level. The following routine details should be clearly indicated:

— title
— author
— date
— acknowledgements
— contents page (with numbers for each chunk)
— index
— glossary.

But other things are often needed:

— a list of the contents of the package, to enable the learner to check its completeness
— instructions on what to do with each part of the package.

This last point is particularly important. Open-learning packages increasingly include a variety of elements. There are several reasons for this: to ensure greater interest, to cater for practical work and to provide several different routes to achieving objectives. The package on marketing produced by AnCO, the Irish Industrial Authority, for example, consists of

# A final postscript

Enjoy your computer; experiment with it. Let your children use it — they cannot harm it either.

Five-year-old children playing a game on the computer

To continue to get the most out of your machine, join a computer club (your local computer store should be able to give you information on any in your area), or read a computing magazine now and then. These will give you new ideas and keep you up-to-date on new products. Many clubs are a good source of low-priced programs.

# Check yourself

Try to apply what you have just learned.

- Go through the five steps on defining your own needs on page 1 to define your own needs for a personal computer.

- Go through the nine steps on page 7 to decide which computer is most suitable for you.

**LOOKING BACK**

1.  Complete this diagram describing the operations between page proofs and final proofs in the system I've described in this course. Explain the role of the type-setter and designer and use arrows to indicate the movements of the proofs and typeset pages. Then compare your diagram with mine.

> The *copyeditor* sends marked page proofs to typesetter.

> The *designer* . . .

> The *typesetter* . . .

2.  What two checks should you make on final proofs?
3.  What does 'passing for press' mean?

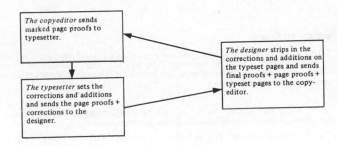

> The *copyeditor* sends marked page proofs to typesetter.

> The *typesetter* sets the corrections and additions and sends the page proofs + corrections to the designer.

> The *designer* strips in the corrections and additions on the typeset pages and sends final proofs + page proofs + typeset pages to the copy-editor.

2.  *See* p. 82
3.  *See* p. 82

**WHAT CAN YOU DO?**

The various stages of proof correction and the movement of proofs between the members of the production team can seem complex at first. Don't worry: it does get simpler the more you do it. Check through the following and if you need help with anything please ask your tutor when you send in your last assignment.

tick

Can you:

1.  decide which of an author's corrections to incorporate into your marked page proofs;   ☐

2.   list the operations between galley proofs and page proofs;   □
3.   list four kinds of errors found in page proofs;   □
4.   list two checks to make on page proofs;   □
5.   list two additions to make to page proofs;   □
6.   list the operations between page proofs and final proofs;   □
7.   list three final checks you must make before 'passing for press'?   □

## ASSIGNMENT F

### Part 1

Take Sheet 6f (i–v) from the wallet. These are five folios from an actual Law 'O' level course currently being prepared by NEC. They need to be copyedited. Mark these up according to the house style on p. 32 and using Hart's *Rules* for any additional information. Send the marked-up pages to your tutor together with any queries you have on this unit.

### Part 2

You'll be aware that in preparing this course we've had to go through all the production processes I've described in the course. What I'd like you to do for the second part of your final assignment is to go through this course book carefully looking for any errors that we've missed! These may have arisen either at the copyediting or proofreading stage. Obviously I hope you don't find any but this course has been complex to produce and you may well be able to find several. Send a list of these errors to your tutor who'll in turn pass them on to us so that we can amend the course when it is reprinted. Can I thank you now for the part you'll play in making sure that this course is presented as accurately as possible in the future.

## WHERE TO NOW?

For an advanced study of copyediting and proofreading I recommend *Copy-editing* by Judith Butcher, Cambridge University Press price £25. This is the book which no professional copyeditor or proofreader can do without. It's expensive but will prove invaluable to you over the years.

If you would like to study further in the field of publishing, the following bodies run courses, some by correspondence, others in college classes:

The Rapid Results College, Tuition House, London SW19 4DS. Tel: 01-947 7272

The Publishers' Association, Book House, 45 East Hill, London SW18 2QE. Tel: 01-874 2718/4608

Oxford Polytechnic, Headington, Oxford OX3 0BP.  Tel: 0865-64777

---

Answers to crossword on p. 35:

Across:   1. detail,   3. paras,   5. MA,   6. list,   7. red,   9. etc.   10. at,   11. transpose,   13. eye,   17. dot, 19. is correct,   22. i.e.   23. Aim,   24. pen,   25. team,   26. Go,   27. rules,   28. skills.

Down:   1. Delete,   2. insert,   3. Parts,   4. style,   6. l.c.,   8. duo,   10. ans,.   12. PO,   14. to,   15. are, 16. a check,   18. time is,   19. incur,   20. cap,   21. rings,   23. a.m.

*Extract from 'Editing for Everyone' by Celia Hall, pp 82, 83, published by and reproduced by permission of the National Extension College*

— eight booklets
— two videotapes
— two audiotapes
— eight sets of MAIL questions (MAIL is a system for providing computer feedback)
— 24 business case-studies.

The Southtek project is even more elaborate.

---

**What will a SOUTHTEK Learning Package look like?**

Before we turn to the detail of the timetable to produce a
SOUTHTEK package, let's have a look at the contents of a
SOUTHTEK Learning Package.  A SOUTHTEK trainee will receive
the materials for which he or she has registered as a Learning
Package, and this will contain many of the elements of the
learning process.  The box or binder containing the package
will be a rigid plastic folder we can send by post.  Inside
it will be some or all of the following:

- a workbook containing the bulk of the printed part of the
learning material.  This will be about 50 pages long and begins
with a description of the package and the way it is organized
for learning.  Study time for each package will be approximately
16 hours

- a practical book containing the exercises to be carried out
with the practical kit provided plus notes or diagrams to
audiovisual material

- first and second progress checks and 'MAIL' test where
applicable

- an audiocassette

- materials for assembly, practical kit or such device as the
basis of practical work.

NB  Some items are optional and may not be included in all
packages.

---

*Extract from an internal document of the Southtek Open Tech project, reproduced by permission
of Southtek Ltd*

The above list refers to what the Southtek learner actually gets at home. 'Package'
can be more widely defined to include those elements delivered by other means. The
following examples, from Southtek, the OU and the YMCA, make this clear.

---

- audiovisual material in video form: this will be supplied
directly to Support Centres in appropriate formats for use on
viewing equipment installed there

- final achievement test format: some briefing on this may be
included in the learning package but not enough to allow the
trainee to 'rig' the test in advance.  Achievement test answers
and the method of applying the tests will be part of the ADVISER
GUIDE

- tutorial support from advisers: this includes both telephone
and face-to-face access, as well as fast turn-round responses
on tests.  These will be typically two tests plus the final
achievement test based on the performance objectives

- practical work facilities, where these do not consist of a
home kit: these facilities will be specified in the adviser
guide together with the specification for the practical work
itself.

---

*Extract from an internal document of the Southtek Open Tech project, reproduced by permission
of Southtek Ltd*

the courses were similar to others produced by the OU in that they used a range of linked components including broadcasting. The course 'package' comprised:

— eight × 32-page full-colour structural learning booklets (with the magazine-style format)

— a 'Jackdaw'-type resource pack containing leaflets, posters and cardboard cutouts
— a computer-marked assignment booklet
— three × 20-minute 'floppy' records
— four × 20-minute radio programmes (on VHF)
— four × 20 TV programmes (on BBC2).

*Extract from 'The Open University Health Education Programme' in 'Open Learning in Action,' Open Learning Guide 1, edited by Roger Lewis, pp 118, 119, published by the Council for Educational Technology*

What actually drops on to a student's doormat is a padded bag containing

— a boxed and labelled audiocassette
— perhaps a set book (on loan)
— a workpack.

The workpack looks like this:

— glossy white cover in light card, printed with the course logo and a window in the front
— through the window you can read the title of the module, the block and the workpack number
— A4 cover and pages, twin hole-punched for ring-binders
— pages attached to the cover by 'treasury tags'.

We have used this format because

— it is cheap and easy to package as the pages come off the collator
— the package lies flat at every page
— the student can file the whole pack as received or refile the items according to his own system.

Workpacks contain 'bread' items and 'meat' items in a sandwich. 'Bread' items will be

— overviews of a new study block (see page 213 for an example)
— a contents list and study schedule planner (see page 214 for an example)
— specification of course requirements
— guidelines on undertaking long-term pieces of project work
— a feedback sheet
— brief extracts from articles of professional interest.

'Meat' items are the teaching elements of the workpack.

*Extract from 'The YMCA Distance-Learning Scheme' in 'Open Learning in Action', Open Learnimg Guide 1, edited by Roger Lewis, p 212, published by the Council for Educational Technology*

With packages of this complexity clear explanations for use are very important. How many parts are there? What is the purpose of each? When, where and how should it be used? How long might it take to study? When he gets a package the learner must know where to look first. The Dundee College of Education Diploma in Educational Technology course uses a sheet — known affectionately as 'a purple' because it is printed on purple. This acts as a guide to the rest of the package, which may contain cassette tapes and a filmstrip as well as print. The 'purple' is always packed last and lies on the top of any box or wallet of materials. Some similar kind of 'read first' element will need to be incorporated in anything but the simplest package.

Some courses produce a separate introduction to the course. The learner keeps this by him throughout. It lists important information such as

— main contacts
— useful telephone numbers
— appeals procedure
— general administration

and often covers

— study skills suggestions
— an explanation of the course structure
— an explanation of any basic terms used (eg, 'self-assessment question', 'activity')
— guidance on any alternative routes through the package.

It may also include questions and assignments. Such a guide is a packaged equivalent of the face-to-face induction often provided on the first day of course attendance.

## A | Activity

Design your package using this section and the material in Sections Five and Six ('Format and layout' and 'How to get started') as necessary. Decide what features each chunk of your package will have:

— at the beginning
— in-text
— at the ending.

If necessary, design a guide on how to use the package.

(If you are selecting a ready-made package rather than producing your own, adapt the activity and following checklist accordingly.)

## C | Checklist

Has your package been organized in manageable learning chunks?

Have you decided what to call the various levels of your package?

Are the various levels of your package integrated? (See the diagrams on page 30 and page 98.)

Are the different parts of each chunk clearly related to one another?

*Beginnings*
Have you devised a standard format for the beginning of each chunk of learning?

Which of the features listed on page 32 will you use?

*In-text*
Have you used the interactive features of open learning? (See page 37); Section One, 'What's so special about open learning materials?' and Section Five, 'Format and layout'.)

Have you decided the points made on page 40 about headings?

Have you used enough signposts? (See page 40.)

*Endings*
Have you devised a standard format for the end of each chunk of learning?

Which of the features listed on page 41 will you use?

*The package as a whole*
Have you given full details of the package? (See page 41.)

Have you provided instructions on how to use the package? (See page 41.)

Do you need a separate course introduction? (See page 47.)

*Section Three. Writing for Learning*

# Writing for Learning

**INTRODUCTION**

No one can learn for another person. The good teacher will stimulate the learner to activity, he will get the learner to commit himself, and to make — and learn from — mistakes. How can this be achieved outside the cut-and-thrust of the classroom?

This section falls into two parts. Firstly, we suggest some methods a writer can use to create and maintain a high level of learner activity. Secondly we give guidelines on how to write prose that will interest and engage the learner to the full.

## Objectives

When you have worked through this section you should be able to

— set work that the learner can manage
— use strategies for helping the learner with difficult material
— use questions and activities in your package
— choose an appropriate tone in which to address the learner
— identify what affects the readability of a package
— write readable prose
— check your prose for readability.

**HOW TO ENCOURAGE ACTIVE LEARNING**

### Set a realistic workload

Learners often turn off because they cannot cope with the sheer bulk of a package. Too often the material takes longer to master than the writer intended. Not enough time is allowed for all the things the learner is asked to do within the package — not only reading but also thinking, note-taking, finding equipment and setting it up, answering questions, carrying out tasks, studying illustrations. And then there are usually activities outside the package itself, such as tutorials, projects, assignments and self-help groups. The learner has to find time for all these things.

### Deal positively with difficult material

There will inevitably be certain parts of your course that learners will find difficult. These may be concepts or skills or processes. What can you do to help the learner with these? Here are some ideas.

Firstly, you should recognize the difficulty. This will be easier if you regularly teach learners similar to those for whom your package is intended. Packages are sometimes written by people who are not in touch with relevant learners. It is all too easy to forget the difficulties involved in learning something new. The following extract shows a recognition of difficulty.

---

One further study note before we move on. In only a few lines of your set book we hit a lot of difficult language; this is an experience you will often have to face as a serious student. There are three reasons for this difficulty. The first is nothing to do with you. In spite of what the back cover of Halsey says (that the book is 'free of jargon') parts of the text are (in our view) unnecessarily difficult, i.e. the writer himself complicates things for you, the reader, by writing in an unclear way. (We can't understand what 'stratified diffusion' means, for example.) The other two sources of difficulty are:

- abstract language generally;
- words used only in social science or with specific 'social science' meanings.

---

*Extract from 'Preparing for Social Science' by Liz Maynard and Roger Lewis, pp 36, 37, published by and reproduced by permission of the National Extension College*

Secondly, keep the introduction of new concepts and operations to a minimum. Introduce only those strictly necessary to the achievement of the objectives. Make sure that each concept is fully explained and illustrated. Often you need to give more than one example. It is through examples that learners relate the new to what is familiar.

---

The cardiovascular system, for instance, may be described in plumbing terms. Although this approach sometimes causes raised academic eyebrows we are determined not to be wooed away from it by accusations that we are reducing the text to a 'Mickey Mouse' level.

---

*Extract from 'Leicester Pharmacy Project' in 'Open Learning in Action', Open Learning Guide 1, edited by Roger Lewis, pp 104, 105, published by the Council for Educational Technology*

**Use questions and activities**
Good self-assessment questions and activities maintain interest and involvement. Volume 2, *How to Help Learners Assess Their Progress*, shows you how to write these.

**Choose the right style and tone**
A friendly approach encourages the learner to be active and to persevere with the difficult tasks of thinking and trying out something new. Here is an example.

# SECTION 2

# ORGANISING YOUR STUDIES

## INTRODUCTION

I want you to think of this course of study as a journey, even an adventure, perhaps into new and challenging territory. You probably have a clearly understood destination — the satisfactory completion of your course, leading to a sucessful examination result. You also have a rough indication of the route, a sketch map if you like, in the form of a syllabus and its set books. What you need to think about now is the best way of making this journey, how best to equip yourself and how best to plan the route. Do not be deterred at this stage, incidentally, if you are following a course of study for its own sake, and are not at all concerned with a qualification. Your journey will be all the more exciting because of its challenging and unpredictable nature.

To equip yourself properly for this journey you need to think about the following questions:

- Where am I starting from in terms of experience, ability and strength of motivation?
- Where should I be aiming to get to?
- How should I plan my studies?
- How do I keep myself going?

*Before reading on any further jot down very briefly your answers to the first question. Be positive: think about your strengths and what you have gained from any previous study of literature.*

*Extract from 'English Literature Study Guide for O-Level Students' by Bernard Jarvis, p 15, published and reproduced by permission of the National Extension College*

It is possible to recreate the friendly, informal tone of a good classroom within the package. Compare these two ways of saying the same thing.

> The answers to the self-check questions are appended below.
> In order to maximise the learning opportunities from this book,
> you must attempt again any questions to which you supplied a
> wrong answer.  If, after repeated attempts of the same questions
> you are still not able to get the correct answer, you ought to
> seek other help.  It is suggested that you contact an Adult
> Literacy and Numeracy Centre in your area or make use of the
> supplications of a friend or colleague.

! answers !

Here are the answers so that you can check
your own work.
If you have got it wrong, think about it and try again.
If it is still wrong ask for help
from a friend or your local Adult Literacy
and Numeracy Centre.

*Extract from 'Make it Count' by Bob Laxton and Graham Rawlinson, p 93, published by and reproduced by permission of the National Extension College*

The latter is a much more appropriate tone to use to address the target learners (in this case, adults unused to studying and possibly lacking confidence).

Opposite is an extract from a package intended for a different group — GPs and non-specialist doctors. The tone is concise and authoritative, appropriate for busy professional people.

But what tone do you use if, as is often the case, you are trying to appeal to a diverse audience who bring to the materials different levels of experience? It is all too tempting to write at the level of the most experienced or able reader. Tempting because then your colleagues are likely to applaud you. But you are writing not for your colleagues, nor for the most able, but for all your target learners. Writers often worry about 'talking down' or seeming patronising, but this is rarely a problem. Experienced learners can look after themselves and skip. Those with less experience and knowledge can work slowly and, encouraged by the friendly tone, successfully absorb the material at a slower rate. So: write for the person who may have to struggle.

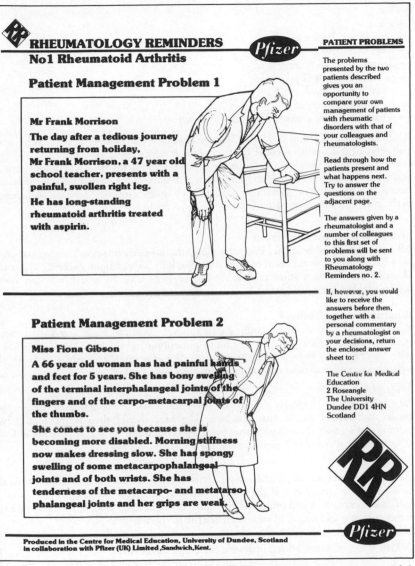

**RHEUMATOLOGY REMINDERS**

**No1 Rheumatoid Arthritis**

**Patient Management Problem 1**

*Pfizer*

**PATIENT PROBLEMS**

The problems presented by the two patients described gives you an opportunity to compare your own management of patients with rheumatic disorders with that of your colleagues and rheumatologists.

Read through how the patients present and what happens next. Try to answer the questions on the adjacent page.

The answers given by a rheumatologist and a number of colleagues to this first set of problems will be sent to you along with Rheumatology Reminders no. 2.

If, however, you would like to receive the answers before then, together with a personal commentary by a rheumatologist on your decisions, return the enclosed answer sheet to:

The Centre for Medical Education
2 Roseangle
The University
Dundee DD1 4HN
Scotland

**Mr Frank Morrison**

The day after a tedious journey returning from holiday, Mr Frank Morrison, a 47 year old school teacher, presents with a painful, swollen right leg.

He has long-standing rheumatoid arthritis treated with aspirin.

**Patient Management Problem 2**

**Miss Fiona Gibson**

A 66 year old woman has had painful hands and feet for 5 years. She has bony swelling of the terminal interphalangeal joints of the fingers and of the carpo-metacarpal joints of the thumbs.

She comes to see you because she is becoming more disabled. Morning stiffness now makes dressing slow. She has spongy swelling of some metacarpophalangeal joints and of both wrists. She has tenderness of the metacarpo- and metatarso-phalangeal joints and her grips are weak.

*Pfizer*

Produced in the Centre for Medical Education, University of Dundee, Scotland in collaboration with Pfizer (UK) Limited ,Sandwich,Kent.

*Extract from 'Rheumatology Reminders', published by and reproduced by permission of the Centre for Medical Education, Dundee*

How do you achieve the right tone? The first and most important piece of advice is to write for somebody in particular, rather than for the world in general. Define a typical learner, give him flesh and blood. Write down details of this imaginary learner, such as

— sex
— age
— educational background
— level of motivation
— degree of visual literacy
— possible study-skill problems
— social background
— hobbies and interests
— what else his life consists of, besides your scheme.

If you have read Volume 5, *How to Develop and Manage an Open-Learning Scheme*, you will remember a similar exercise for the course developer.

Once you have sketched out an image of the target learner then you can write as if you were speaking personally to him. The word 'speaking' is particularly appropriate since, as we stressed in 'What's so special about open-learning?', you are recreating, in the package, the to-and-fro of classroom conversation.

### HOW TO WRITE READABLE PROSE

All prose should be readable, but particularly the prose in an open-learning package — whether this is in the form of text, soundtrack or on a computer screen. This part identifies issues which affect readability and suggests ways by which you can assess how readable your own writing is.

### What affects readability?

You need to think about tone; paragraphing; sentence length and structure; vocabulary; and other ways than prose of presenting information. We dealt earlier with tone; here we consider the other points. We give guidelines which, as with all such advice, you will need to modify to suit your own context.

### Paragraphing

Paragraphs should be clearly structured. There should be one idea in each paragraph, usually introduced in the first sentence. The idea should then be supported by examples. It's generally reckoned that paragraphs should be no longer than about five to seven lines, about 65–91 words (assuming 13 words to a line).

### Sentences

Ideally, sentences are short and simply structured, with one idea in each. Difficult ideas are easier to absorb if they are embedded in simple sentences. You should restrict sentences to a maximum of 20 words. There should, though, be some variety in the structure and length of sentences. See the following examples.

| | |
|---|---|
| SIMPLE ↓ COMPLEX | Open-learning materials challenge the learner. |
| | Open-learning materials challenge the learner and at the same time reassure him. |
| | Open-learning materials, which are time-consuming to construct, challenge the learner. |
| | Open-learning materials, which are time-consuming to construct, challenge the learner and at the same time reassure him, because the writer's tone is always personal. |

*Vocabulary*
You should use short, simple and familiar words wherever possible (see examples on pages 58 and 59). Sometimes you have to introduce technical terms. You should define and illustrate these and give the learner a chance to use them, as in the following example.

---

In Block 1, Unit 3 we considered the housewife deciding to spend her limited amount of money on a small number of (expensive) strawberries or a larger number of (cheaper) oranges. What fixes these prices? According to supply and demand, the price is determined by the amount produced for sale on the one hand and, on the other, the amount people want to buy. This can be applied to the market for people as well as to that for goods; we use the expression 'labour market' in everyday discussion.

**SAQ 1:** What do you think the 'labour market' means?

Labour is bought and sold, just like kippers and digital watches, in the market place. People sell their labour at the price (which we call a wage) which the employer is prepared to pay. The scarcer the skill or capacity the higher the price is likely to be.

**SAQ 2:** Can you apply this principle to the GP and the shop assistant and use it to explain why the GP is paid so much more?

Supply and demand would explain it as follows: there are not so many doctors and so they have a higher 'market value' than shop assistants. Another way of putting this is to say that there are more people who possess the skills needed to become shop assistants than there are those who possess the skills that qualify them to become doctors.

**SAQ 3:** Why are there fewer doctors than shop assistants?

Before someone becomes a doctor he or she has to undergo a long period of training to acquire the necessary skills.
This is how the theory of supply and demand helps us to understand the different rates of pay. But (like most theories) this one has to be modified when further evidence is considered. It is also a fact, for example, that the doctors' trade union

---

*Extract from 'Preparing for Social Science' by Liz Maynard and Roger Lewis, p 65, published by and reproduced by permission of the National Extension College*

*Negatives*
You should use negatives with great care. It is much easier for the learner to take in a positive statement than the same statement put in a negative way. Compare 'It is much easier to absorb a positive than a negative emphasis' with 'It is much harder to absorb a negative than a positive emphasis'; or 'Negatives should be used with great care' with 'Negatives should not be used carelessly'. Double negatives are particularly unhelpful. Compare 'You can easily see . . .' with 'It is not unusual to see . . .'; or 'The Red Admiral is common in East Anglia' with 'The Red Admiral is not uncommon in East Anglia'.

| Wordy English | Better English |
|---|---|
| due to the fact that | because |
| it is apparent therefore that | hence |
| in all other cases | otherwise |
| it may well be that | perhaps |
| by the same token | similarly |
| with the result that | so |
| is not in a position to | cannot, can't |
| in connection with | about |
| with regard to | about |
| in order to | to |
| in conjunction with | with |
| in spite of the fact that | although |
| make an adjustment to | adjust |
| arrive at a decision | decide |
| give positive encouragement to | encourage |
| make an examination of | examine |
| bring to a conclusion | finish |
| undertake a study of | study |
| try out | try |
| make an attempt to | try |
| at an early date | soon |
| if it is assumed that | if |
| with the exception of | except |
| entertainment value | fun |
| in the vicinity of | near |
| a small number of | few |
| a high degree of | much |
| a proportion of | some |
| prior to | before |
| at a later date | later |
| have been shown to be | are |
| take into consideration | consider |
| come to the conclusion that | conclude |
| at that point in time | then |
| in this day and age | today |
| until such time as | until |
| in most cases | usually |
| are found to be in agreeement | agree |

*Avoid trendiness, jargon, clichés, etc*

| Long word | Short word |
|---|---|
| accelerate | speed up |
| accomplish | do |
| acquaint, appraise | tell |
| advantageous | useful |
| alleviate | ease |
| anticipate | expect |
| approximately | about |
| ascertain | find out |
| assistance | help |
| commence | begin |
| component | part |
| consequently | so |
| deficiency | lack of |
| demonstrate | show |
| dominant, predominant | main |
| donate | give |
| emphasize | stress |
| endeavour | try |
| expenditure | spending |
| facilitate | ease; help |
| firstly | first |
| forward | send |
| frequently | often |
| generate | produce; give |
| initiate | start |
| investigate | look into |
| locate | find |
| manufacture | make |
| methodology | methods |
| modification | change |
| nevertheless | but; however |
| opportunity | chance |
| personnel | people |
| principal | main |
| proportion | part |
| purchase | buy |
| regarding | about |
| represents | is |
| subsequently | later |
| terminate | end |
| utilize | use |
| virtually | almost |

*Use short words rather than long*

*Passive and impersonal*
You should use these with care. Avoid them whenever possible. Address the learner directly — 'I' to 'you'. Compare 'You should now turn to your home experiment kit' with 'It is now necessary for the learner to turn to his home experiment kit'; or 'I am now coming to a difficult topic' with 'It is now time to deal with a difficult topic'.

As usual there are exceptions. Some groups of learners will be put off by a personal approach. But most writers are too formal. When I had finished the first draft of this section I was embarrassed to find that I had used the impersonal throughout rather than addressing you directly, eg, 'individual words should wherever possible be short and familiar' instead of 'You should use short and familiar words wherever possible'.

*Means other than prose*
You should use these wherever possible. Lists, graphs and the other visual devices are discussed in the section on Illustrations (page 69).

*Number of words*
You should keep these to a minimum but remember that sometimes words can help the learner. Words spent giving an example, relating an experience or giving reassurance are perceived as helpful; words which merely introduce yet more inert information create a feeling of overload. So keep words to a minimum, but don't begrudge those which support the learner.

---

Problems of vocabulary are obviously most common with poetry written several centuries ago, such as Milton's and, as we shall see, Shakespeare's. But modern poetry can be difficult too. Look at these two lines, for example, from a twentieth-century poem *On a Raised Beach* by Hugh McDiarmid:

All is lithogenesis — or lochia,
Carpolite fruit of the forbidden tree.

I certainly needed a dictionary to tackle that! In fact, I needed a dictionary larger than the one I had at home, and had to go to the library to look the words up. You will probably need to do this yourself in some instances, and I suggest you make a list of words to look up on each visit. The *Shorter Oxford* dictionary is probably the one best suited to your needs in this course. So be prepared to work at the poems which you choose to read closely or which you are required to study during an exam or for an essay. You will need to read these poems several times and at least one of these readings should be aimed at understanding the meaning. George MacBeth gives some helpful advice on this:

---

*Extract from 'Companion Guide to Poetry for O-Level Students' by Roger Lewis, p 23, published by and reproduced by permission of the National Extension College*

**A**

**Activity**
First read the passage on page 62 aloud. Then answer the following questions.

(a) Did you find this easy?

(b) Can you find any impersonal/passive uses of language?

(c) Underline all the words of three or more syllables.

(d) Count the words in the longest sentence. Could any of the material be presented in another way than continuous prose?

(e) Does any of the passage use words to support you, the reader?

Then check your response with what follows.

(a) You probably found the passage difficult read aloud. In particular, you probably found the long sentence in the middle of paragraph 5 impossible to read fluently. The prose does not flow and would be disastrous if adopted in an open-learning text. The remaining work you have done on the passage should help you to see why.

(b) There are many examples. Here are just two: 'it may be possible to'; 'it should be appreciated, however'.

(c) There are a great many words of three or more syllables. As a rule of thumb you can take this as an indication of the proportion of difficult words in the passage — difficult in meaning, difficult to recognize, or uncommon.

(d) The longest sentence begins 15 lines into paragraph 2. It begins 'In areas where there are only one or two . . .' and ends 'or teachers of the deaf/blind'. The sentence has 84 or 85 words, depending on whether you count deaf-blind as one or two. It is much too long. You may feel that it would be better presented in a flowchart or similar format. If not, at least it should be broken down into shorter sentences. It has (we think — it's hard to disentangle) one main clause and five subsidiary ones. There is generally no need to write sentences with more than three clauses.

(e) Little or no concession is made to the reader. The writer concentrates only on the content.

4.  The development of children with handicaps of sight and
hearing is much slower than that of other children.  It may be
a number of years before a firm decision can be reached as to
the kind of special educational treatment most suitable to the
child's needs and the extent to which he is capable of
benefiting from it.  His development will need, therefore, to
be carefully followed and his needs and capacity kept under
review at regular intervals from an early age.  Persons
experienced in education, medicine and other appropriate
disciplines should take part in this continuing assessment.
Authorities should be aware of the facilities available at the
specialist assessment centre at the Royal National Institute
for the Blind unit at Condover Hall, where these children live
at the unit for a short time whilst being assessed.

5.  The small numbers of these children, as compared with the
total school population, their scattered distribution and the
variety of different types of care they need, make arrangements
for their education very difficult.  The most effective
placement in the early stages will depend not only on the
extent and nature of the child's disabilities but also on the
location of his home.  In densely populated urban areas it may
be possible to assemble a number of children to form a special
nursery or infant class, perhaps with other handicapped
children, and possibly in association with an existing special
school.  Experience with existing groups of this kind suggests
that they should consist of not more than 6 children with
defects of sight and hearing, each group being in the charge of
a suitably qualified teacher assisted by 2 ancillary workers.
In areas where there are only one or 2 of these children,
consideration may be given to placing them, subject to
satisfactory arrangements being made, individually in ordinary
nursery schools or classes, special schools or units, or (where
they are suffering in addition from mental handicap) in junior
training centres, utilising suitable specialist help that is
locally available such as speech therapists, peripatetic
teachers of the deaf, teachers from schools for the deaf, for
the blind or partially sighted, or teachers of the deaf/blind.
Where an existing nursery school or class, or training centre
admits one of these children, consideration should be given to
the addition of one person to the staff who would accept
particular responsibility for the care of the child and all
staff should be informed about the problems involved.  If none
of these alternatives is available or considered suitable,
specialist educational support should be provided wherever
possible for the child at home.  It should be appreciated,
however, that there is a cumulative strain, physical as well as
mental, on parents looking after these children at home and
every effort should be made to organise relief for them.

## How to check readability

There are at least four ways of checking the readability of what you have written.
Each in its own way is limited, but taken together they can give you a useful guide.
And they need take only a little of your time. The ways are: using a checklist
yourself; using a colleague or learner; using the Cloze test, and using a readability

formula. Of these, using a learner is possibly the most important and Volume 7, *How to Manage the Production Process,* gives detailed guidance on how to do this.

### Using a checklist

The checklist on pages 65–6 gives questions you might ask yourself to check your writing. The techniques suggested in this section and in the checklist will help you to spot any problems you may have. You can then work at them and get them right. It is best to leave a gap between writing your work and checking it. You can then look at it more objectively.

Writing habits, like any other habits, can be changed if you work at it systematically. This is well worth doing if you want to write effective open-learning materials.

### Using a colleague/learner

A powerful way of testing your material is simply to sit beside a colleague or, preferably, a learner to see how long it takes him to read through it and ask him to mark any words or phrases which he finds difficult or unusual. This can be used in conjunction with the other methods. Developmental testing with learners is discussed further in Volume 7, *How to Manage the Production Process.*

### The Cloze test

Take a passage of your own text about 250 words long. Leave a 35-word run-in and then delete the 36th word and every tenth word thereafter (46th, 56th, 66th, 76th, etc). Stop deleting words when you have deleted 20. An easy way to blank out the words is simply to stick a disguise of Blutak on the top. It's better if the reader doesn't know the length of the missing word. But this would mean specially preparing the passage and is probably not worth the trouble in this case.

Now select one (or several) of the people in your target group of learners and try it out.

If he (they) fail to provide the *correct* word or a *totally acceptable alternative* in at least 13 cases out of the 20, then the text is too difficult.

If this *is* the result then modify the passage by simplifying the language, shortening the sentences and avoiding the use of long or difficult words.

### A readability formula

There are several formulae you could use. We introduce here one which we have found useful — the Modified Fog Index. (You will, by the way, find that these tests usually have bizarre names.) This is how to use the Modified Fog Index.

Take a sample of about 100 words (several samples would give a better guide but would take too much time).

Count all the long words (three syllables or more) in the sample and then work out the average sentence length of the *complete* sentences within the sample. Then apply this formula.

$$\frac{(\text{average sentence length} + \text{long words}) \times 2}{5} + 5 = \text{reading age}$$

Thus, if the average sentence length was 20 words and there were four long words,

$$\frac{(20 + 4) \times 2}{5} + 5 = ra$$

$$\frac{48}{5} + 5 = ra$$

$$9.6 + 5 = ra$$

Reading age = 14.6 — ie, the passage is suitable for the average reader of 14.6 years. A score above 20 indicates that the text is for the highly literate, and may well be hard for anyone.

**Checking readability: an example**
The following activity gives you a chance to try out this advice.

**Activity**
Turn back to the passage on page 62.

(a) Prepare the passage for Cloze testing as described on page 63). Try it out on a colleague. Remember that if he fails to supply the correct word or a totally acceptable alternative in at least 13 cases out of 20, then the text is too difficult.

(b) Use the Modified Fog Index as described on page 63 on at least the first paragraph of the passage. Then compare your results with ours given below.

Here are our findings, for (b), the first paragraph of the passage.

The sentences are 18, 40, 24, 16 and 39 words long, so the average sentence length is $\frac{137}{5}$, ie, approx 27.

There are 27 words of three syllables or more. The formula thus reads

$$\frac{(27 + 27) \times 2}{5} + 5 = ra$$

$$\frac{108}{5} + 5 = ra$$

$$21.6 + 5 = ra$$

Reading age = 26.6

These tests provide only a rough guide to reading level and it is easy to see their limitations (eg, some words of three syllables — such as Condover in our example — are really quite simple). They do nevertheless give us a quick indication of the level of difficulty of our writing.

Two further points need mentioning.

Both tests work with passages of continuous prose. In most open-learning texts, such passages form only part of the material. Exercises, questions, lists, tables, headings, instructions are interspersed with prose. Readability tests do not tell us much about these aspects: in particular, they do not tell us how well readers can follow instructions we give. So a suitable score on a number of tests does not necessarily mean that our writing is clear enough.

Some tests necessarily contain a number of long words which are technical terms. It is advisable here to use Cloze tests with learners studying the subject at the right level. We should also check that each technical term is explained fully the first time it is used and that learners are given a chance to use this word themselves, eg, in a self-assessment question.

---

We have evolved a set of stylistic conventions. The only conscious decision we made was always to write 'he/she' or 's/he' when we wanted to refer to a single person of either sex. We address the student frequently, always as 'you', singular. The author always uses 'I' except when the course team is specifically meant. We try to keep sentences short, with no more than one subordinate clause. Paragraphs are kept short as well.

In the early stages we were very vigilant about use of technical terms and we also made use of formal tests of readability — the Cloze Test and the Fog Factor, for instance. We now leave it to the editor to spot errors of this sort intuitively. We may be getting a bit careless at this stage but I think by the middle of the course students can cope with this. Footnotes are absolutely forbidden.

---

*Extract from 'The YMCA Distance-Learning Scheme', Open Learning Guide 1, edited by Roger Lewis, p 217, published by the Council for Educational Technology*

## A

**Activity**

Take a section of your text.

Check how well you are helping your client to learn by using the checklist below.

You can also apply the checklist to a ready-made package you are considering using in the scheme.

## C

**Checklist**

*How to encourage active learning*

Have you set a realistic workload?

Have you kept difficult material down to an absolute minimum?

Are your expectations of the learner realistic?

Have you fully explained and illustrated difficult material?

Have you used enough self-assessment questions and activities?

Is your style and approach friendly?

Have you used an appropriate tone?

*How to write readable prose*
*Paragraphing.* Does each paragraph contain one main idea?

Is this idea supported by the rest of the paragraph?

Are your paragraphs short (5–7 lines maximum)?

*Sentences.* Are any sentences too long or complex?

Are any sentences more than 20 words long?

*Vocabulary.* Have you used too many long words?

Have you used too many technical words?

Have you defined and explained any technical terms you must use?

Have you used any unnecessary jargon?

Have you used any trendy or 'pet' words?

*Negatives/passive and impersonal.* Have you used negatives with care?

Have you used the passive and impersonal with care?

*Means other than prose.* Have you used means other than prose to present content and to support learning?

*Number of words.* Have you kept the number of words down to the minimum?

*Checking your prose.* Have you checked your prose

— yourself, using a checklist
— using a colleague
— using a learner
— using the Cloze procedure
— using a readability formula?

Have you made any necessary changes to your manuscript in the light of the checks?